IMAGINATIVE PRAYER TEMPLATES

IMAGINATIVE PRAYER TEMPLATES

Ademola O. Sodeinde

IMAGINATIVE PRAYER TEMPLATES

Publishing Division of Calvary Gathering Ministry

© 2016 by Ademola O. Sodeinde

International Standard Book Number 978-0-9983236-0-2

Scripture quotations of the Holy Bible are from:
English Standard Version (ESV)
King James Version (KJV)
New Century Version (NCV)
New International Version (NIV)
New King James Version (NKJV)
The Amplified (AMP)

Printed in the United States of America

ALL RIGHTS RESERVED

No part of this publication may be reproduced, stored in a retrieval system, or transmitted, in any form or by any means- electronic, mechanical, photocopying, recording, or otherwise- without prior written permission.

For information:

Reverend Ademola O. Sodeinde
Publishing Division of Calvary Gathering Ministry
calvarygatheringministry@gmail.com
http://calvarygatheringmi.wixsite.com/wholeness
https://www.facebook.com/CGMinistry/

To Kelley Sodeinde, wife and partner in ministry, I love you. And to the saints who continually stand in the place of prayer. Blessings.

Contents

Contents	6
Acknowledgements	7
CHAPTER ONE	13
CHAPTER TWO	31
CHAPTER THREE	45
CHAPTER FOUR	53
CHAPTER FIVE	57
CHAPTER SIX	62
CHAPTER SEVEN	65
APPENDIX I	76
APPENDIX II	103
IN CLOSING	113

Acknowledgements

Glory and honor to God, the Almighty, the Creator and to our Savior, Jesus Christ, and to the Holy Spirit. This book was inspired by *A Prayer Time Teaching Moment* I conducted at Mt. Moriah East Baptist Church in Memphis, TN during the summer of 2016 at the invitation of Rev. Dr. Melvin Charles Smith, the Senior Pastor. Thank you for the warm reception and the teachable hearts of the saints in your church. I appreciate you and the congregation.

I would like to express sincere gratitude to members of various congregations, particularly in Memphis, TN where I have served in the Christian ministry as Associate Campus Minister, Minister of Outreach, Founding Minister and

Preacher on Rotation, Adjunct Instructor, Associate Pastor, Pastor and, Chief Servant Caregiver.

There being too many individuals to mention, I will list the congregations: Wesley Foundation, University of Memphis, Longstreet United Methodist Church, "The Gathering" (Colonial Park UMC), Formation for Ministry, Memphis Theological Seminary, New Generation Ministry Empowerment Center, Holy Community United Methodist Church, Calvary Longview United Methodist church and Calvary Gathering Ministry.

I thank my mother, Olori Agba D. O. Sodeinde, who instilled the discipline of family prayer time in me.

Special thanks to Olori Kelley Adeifeoluwa J. Sodeinde, my darling and better half, for her understanding and support, reading the manuscript and giving constructive suggestions. I appreciate and love you.

To Oluwaseyi Adewunmi Sodeinde and Oyindamola Adenike Sodeinde, my darling daughters, I am so proud of you and I thank you.

Special thanks to Kathy Earl, my adopted mother, for taking time to read the manuscript and offering constructive suggestions. You are such a joy.

I cannot close this acknowledgement without the mention of Mama Ernestine Byrd, Tom & Kathy Earl, Ayodele & Hannah Oyebanjo, Bishop Don Jones, Bishop Andre Cross, Rev. Dr. D'Arcy A. Deveaux Sr., Tunde & Toyin Thompson, Bernado & Amanda Zapata, Ann Lawson, Mozell Starks, Charlene Stewart, Mary McGhee, Mattie Bryant, Margaret Hill, Diane Edwards, Winnie Kilzer, Chris Edwards and Tabitha Guy. To each one of you, I am particularly grateful.

God's blessings.

Personal Testimony

I was young, and now I am old, but I have never seen good people left helpless or their children begging for food.[1]

God answers prayers. We just have to ask. *"Ask, and God will give to you. Search, and you will find. Knock, and the door will open for you.*[2] At a very early age I started

---

[1] Psalm 37:25 New Century Version (NCV)

experiencing God as the *'I am'* God who is beautiful for all situations. I experienced God as protector, healer, guide, leader, provider, help, and so on. By God's grace I survived the harsh conditions of a country in civil war and various violent attempts and changes of government through *coup d'états*. I survived many bouts of malaria, cholera epidemic which killed many children my age.

As a student, I remember always praying and God gave me understanding. I experienced God provided guidance through steps of life. Through prayers, jobs were provided, doors of opportunities were opened. God made ways, after all, Jesus *is the way, the truth, and the life.*[3]

When the difficulties of life came, God came through for me. God will come through for all who put their trust in God. I was never alone.[4]

---

[2] Matthew 7:7 New Century Version (NCV)
[3] John 14:6
[4] Keep your lives free from the love of money, and be satisfied with what you have. God has said, "I will never leave you; I will never abandon you." - Hebrews 13:5 New Century Version (NCV)

CHAPTER ONE
Prayers

"Pray continually," - 1 Thessalonians 5:17

A DICTIONARY DEFINITION OF PRAYER IS: *a spiritual communion with God or an object of worship, as in supplication, thanksgiving, adoration, or confession.*[5] Prayer is communication with God, the Almighty, the Creator and Savior! Prayer is worship addressed to the Father, in the name of Jesus Christ, and in the power of the Holy Spirit. We pray to God in the name of Jesus Christ as we are empowered by the Holy Spirit.

---

[5] *See http://www.dictionary.com/browse/prayer*

We are encouraged to pray to God always regardless of our situation. We are to give thanks whatever happens. That is what God wants for us in Christ Jesus.[6]

Sometimes the situation will be good and sometimes the situation will be bad, but God promised to be with us all the way. God is our protection and our strength. He always helps in times of trouble.[7]

However, we may not be in sync with God sometimes because of 'personal issues', which make us wander away of the presence of God.

> Jesus said, *"I told you these things so that you can have peace in me. In this world you will have trouble, but be brave! I have defeated the world."*[8] *"God is our protection and our strength. He always helps in times of trouble. Even if the oceans roar and foam, or the mountains shake at the raging sea. Selah. There is a river that brings joy to the city of God, the holy place where God Most High lives. God is in that city, and so it will not be shaken. God will help her at dawn. Nations tremble and kingdoms shake. God shouts and the earth crumbles. The* LORD *All-Powerful is with us; the God of Jacob is our defender. Selah."*[9]

---

[6] 1 Thessalonians 5:18
[7] Psalm 46:1
[8] John 16:33 New Century Version (NCV)
[9] Psalm 46:1, 3-7 New Century Version (NCV)

God want us to have faith and not fear. We are to put our trust in God. God is actually concerned about us individually. We are to simply cast our burden on the Lord. Hear God speaking, *"So don't worry, because I am with you. Don't be afraid, because I am your God. I will make you strong and will help you; I will support you with my right hand that saves you."*[10]

> We have assurances in God. *"For God did not give us a spirit of timidity (of cowardice, of craven and cringing and fawning fear), but [He has given us a spirit] of power and of love and of calm and well-balanced mind and discipline and self-control."*[11] *"Cast your burden on the Lord [releasing the weight of it] and He will sustain you; He will never allow the [consistently] righteous to be moved (made to slip, fall, or fail)."*[12] *"Casting the whole of your care [all your anxieties, all your worries, all your concerns, once and for all] on Him, for He cares for you affectionately and cares about you watchfully."*[13]

When we pray God responds. *"And this is the boldness we have in God's presence: that if we ask God for anything that agrees with*

---

[10] Isaiah 41:10 New Century Version (NCV)
[11] 2 Tim 1:7 (AMP)
[12] Psalm 55:22 (AMP)
[13] 1 Peter 5:7 (AMP)

what he wants, he hears us. If we know he hears us every time we ask him, we know we have what we ask from him."[14]

We get results. Because God is not a magician or a rubber stamp, God's response to our request is often in tandem to God's will. Focusing on God and not on our worldly cravings will help us to know God's will.[15] God's response to us may be;

Yes. *"Then David asked the LORD, "Should I chase the people who took our families? Will I catch them?" The LORD answered, "Chase them. You will catch them, and you will succeed in saving your families."*[16]

No. *"Then David said to Nathan the prophet, "Look, I am living in a palace made of cedar wood, but the Ark of God is in a tent!" Nathan said to the king, "Go and do what you really want to do, because the LORD is with you." But that night the LORD spoke his word to Nathan, "Go and tell my servant David, 'this is what the LORD says: Will you build a house for me to live in? From the time I brought the Israelites out of Egypt*

---

[14] 1 John 5:14-15 New Century Version (NCV)
[15] "Do not be shaped by this world; instead be changed within by a new way of thinking. Then you will be able to decide what God wants for you; you will know what is good and pleasing to him and what is perfect." Romans 12:1-2 New Century Version (NCV)
[16] 1 Samuel 30:8 New Century Version (NCV)

until now I have not lived in a house. I have been moving around all this time with a tent as my home. "You must tell my servant David, 'this is what the LORD *All-Powerful says: I took you from the pasture and from tending the sheep and made you leader of my people Israel. "When you die and join your ancestors, I will make one of your sons the next king, and I will set up his kingdom. He will build a house for me, and I will let his kingdom rule always."* [17]

Wait. *"It is not yet time for the message to come true, but that time is coming soon; the message will come true. It may seem like a long time, but be patient and wait for it, because it will surely come; it will not be delayed."* [18]

New. *"Look at the new thing I am going to do. It is already happening. Don't you see it? I will make a road in the desert and rivers in the dry land."* [19]

Finally, God's response may just be, silence. " … *The people will not be hungry for bread or thirsty for water, but they will be hungry for words from the* LORD*."* [20]

---

[17] 2 Samuel 7: 2-6, 8,12-13
[18] Habakkuk 2:3 New Century Version (NCV)
[19] Isaiah 43:19 New Century Version (NCV)

Prayer is one of the hardest things to do. Really, if we can help it, we do not want to pray. We would prefer to have it easy, like the disciples and really not have to worry about prayer, especially coupled with fasting.[21] Jesus was physically present with the disciples and maybe because Jesus was doing the heavy lifting work of prayers himself. Jesus often slipped away to be alone so he could pray.[22]

Many reasons could be given to explain why we do not pray enough. These include but are not limited to the following. We are just not interested. We do not see any reason to pray. We are satisfied with the way things are, so much so that we have no desire for change.

We often claim to be too busy. We just don't have the "*time*" to pray. There are already too many activities that we have to attend to. We could be lazy.

---

[20] Amos 8:11 New Century Version (NCV)
[21] Now the followers of John and the Pharisees often fasted for a certain time. Some people came to Jesus and said, "Why do John's followers and the followers of the Pharisees often fast, but your followers don't?" Jesus answered, "The friends of the bridegroom do not fast while the bridegroom is still with them. As long as the bridegroom is with them, they cannot fast. But the time will come when the bridegroom will be taken from them, and then they will fast.- Mark 2:18-20 New Century Version (NCV)
[22] Luke 5:16 New Century Version (NCV)

We lack concern for others because we get so wrapped up in our own lives. Sometimes we are narrow minded in our thinking, we assume that God only cares about our big problems, so we don't attempt to pray about the little ones.

Sometimes we think small, afraid to ask God for bigger things. It could be that we do not like to make commitments. We fail to pray because we are afraid. We quietly tell ourselves, "What will happen if God does answer our prayer?"

We must take time as Christians to pray. We must have love and concern for other people and our world enough to pray! The more we pray, the easier it becomes. The time is now for us to pray and fast.

Because we do not always see instant results should not stop us from praying. God might be seeing things differently from the way we see it and so we have to be patient.

"Just as the heavens are higher than the earth, so are my ways higher than your ways and my thoughts higher than your

thoughts."[23] *"But those who wait on the LORD Shall renew their strength;*

they shall mount up with wings like eagles, they shall run and not be weary, they shall walk and not faint." [24]

Sometimes we find ourselves discouraged and weak. Like the disciples we find ourselves sleeping, *"Then Jesus went back to his followers and found them asleep. He said to Peter, "You men could not stay awake with me for one hour?"* [25] We are in a dark place.

Hear the word of the God; *"Stay awake and pray for strength against temptation. The spirit wants to do what is right, but the body is weak."* [26]

The major obstacle could be sin in our lives. *"If I had known of any sin in my heart, the Lord would not have listened to me."* [27]

Prayer is an essential element in our relationship with the Lord. We can have the confidence to pray when we have a relationship with God.

---

[23] Isaiah 55:9 New Century Version (NCV)
[24] Isaiah 40:31 New King James Version (NKJV)
[25] Matthew 26:40 New Century Version (NCV)
[26] Matthew 26:41 New Century Version (NCV)
[27] Psalm 66:18 New Century Version (NCV)

> *"My sheep listen to my voice; I know them, and they follow me."*[28]
>
> *"And this is the confidence that we have in him, that, if we ask any thing according to his will, he heareth us: And if we know that he hear us, whatsoever we ask, we know that we have the petitions that we desired of him."*[29]

Prayer becomes easier and we have the boldness to approach the throne of grace.

> Hebrews 4:16 declares, *"Let us then approach the throne of grace with confidence, so that we may receive mercy and find grace to help us in our time of need."*[30]

God gives us Mercy and Grace, which are easily confused. Grace and Mercy are not the same.

Mercy is God not punishing us as our sins deserve, and grace is God blessing us despite the fact that we do not deserve it. Mercy is deliverance from judgment. Grace is extending kindness to the unworthy.

This is the word of God,

---

[28] John 10:27 New Century Version (NCV)
[29] 1 John 5:14-15 King James Version (KJV)
[30] Hebrews 4:16 English Standard version (ESV)

"Surely there is not a good person on earth who always does good and never sins."[31] *"Everyone has sinned and fallen short of God's glorious standard,"*[32] *"If we say we have no sin, we are fooling ourselves, and the truth is not in us."*[33]

Because of sin, what we deserve is death. *"The payment for sin is death. But God gives us the free gift of life forever in Christ Jesus our Lord."*[34]

God showed us grace. We are saved by the grace of God.[35] *"Even when we were dead in sins, hath quickened us together with Christ, (by grace ye are saved)."*[36]

Grace is simply defined as unmerited favor. God favors us with good things that we do not deserve and could never earn. It is a free gift of God, paid for with the blood of our Lord Jesus Christ.

---

[31] Ecclesiastes 7:20 New Century Version (NCV)
[32] Romans 3:23 New Century Version (NCV)
[33] 1 John 1:8 New Century Version (NCV)
[34] Romans 6:23 New Century Version (NCV)
[35] For by grace are ye saved through faith; and that not of yourselves: it is the gift of God: Not of works, lest any man should boast. Ephesians 2:8-9 King James Version (KJV)
[36] Ephesians 2:5 King James Version (KJV)

Therefore, *"and all need to be made right with God by his grace, which is a free gift. They need to be made free from sin through Jesus Christ."*[37] *"God loved the world so much that he gave his one and only Son so that whoever believes in him may not be lost, but have eternal life."*[38]

Mercy and grace are best explained by the salvation God gave us through Jesus Christ. Although we deserve judgment, when we receive Jesus Christ as Savior, we receive mercy from God and are delivered from judgment.

Instead of judgment, we receive by grace salvation, forgiveness of sins, abundant life. *"But as many as received Him, to them He gave the right to become children of God, to those who believe in His name:"*[39]

If you are not a child of God, or you are in doubt of your assurance of salvation, now is the time to do something about it.

---

[37] Romans 3:24 New Century Version (NCV)
[38] John 3:16 New Century Version (NCV)
[39] John 1:12 New King James Version (NKJV)

"God says, "*At the right time I heard your prayers. On the day of salvation I helped you.*"[40] "*I tell you that the "right time" is now, and the "day of salvation" is now.*"[41]

Please consider sincerely taking the following steps.

Admit you are a sinner. *"There is no one righteous, not even one ... for all have sinned and fall short of the glory of God."* Romans 3:10, 23. (See Romans 5:8 and 6:23.) Ask God's forgiveness. *"Everyone who calls on the name of the Lord will be saved."* Romans 10:13

Believe in the Lord Jesus Christ. Put your trust in Christ as your only hope of salvation. *"For God so loved the world that he gave his one and only Son, that whoever believes in him shall not perish but have eternal life."* John 3:16 (See John 14:6.). You become a child of God by receiving Jesus Christ. *"To all who receive him, to those who believed in his name, he gave the right to become children of God."* John 1:12 (See Revelation 3:20.)

Confess that Jesus is your Lord. *"If you confess with your mouth, 'Jesus is Lord,' and believe in your heart that God raised him from the dead, you will be saved."* Romans 10:9 (See verse 10.)

---

[40] Isaiah 49:8 New Century Version (NCV)
[41] 2 Corinthians 6:2 New Century Version (NCV)

IMAGINATIVE PRAYER TEMPLATES

Sincerely pray the salvation prayer. You can say or adapt the salvation prayer in your own way. Be sincere. The Salvation Prayer (sometimes referred to as the Sinner's Prayer) below, is not an "official prayer" but rather a sample prayer to follow when asking Jesus into your heart.

You can pray to God in your own words if you choose. The basis of the Sinner's Prayer comes from Romans 10:9-10.

> *"That if thou shalt confess with thy mouth the Lord Jesus, and shalt believe in thine heart that God hath raised him from the dead, thou shalt be saved. For with the heart man believeth unto righteousness; and with the mouth confession is made unto salvation."*

SALVATION PRAYER

"Dear God in heaven, I come to you in the name of Jesus. I acknowledge to you that I am a sinner, and I am sorry for my sins and the life that I have lived; I need your forgiveness.

I believe that your only begotten Son Jesus Christ shed His precious blood on the cross at Calvary and died for my sins, and I am now willing to turn from my sin.

You said in your Holy Word, Romans 10:9 that if we confess the Lord our God and believe in our hearts that God raised Jesus from the dead, we shall be saved.

Right now I confess Jesus as the Lord of my soul. With my heart, I believe that God raised Jesus from the dead. This very moment I accept Jesus Christ as my own personal Savior and according to His Word, right now I am saved.

Thank you Jesus for your unlimited grace which has saved me from my sins. I thank you Jesus that your grace never leads to license, but rather it always leads to repentance. Therefore Lord Jesus transform my life so that I may bring glory and honor to you alone and not to myself.

Thank you Jesus for dying for me and giving me eternal life. AMEN."[42]

Now, start to read and study the word of God, the Holy Bible, starting with the book of John. **Pray asking God to lead you to join a Bible believing Church** near where you live and introduce yourself to the church leadership.

My experience has been that God does indeed answer prayers. Oftentimes my plan is not God's plan, and God's schedule is not my schedule. Accepting God's plan and truly

---

[42] http://salvationprayer.info/home/salvation/

putting God first is difficult, but when I am able to do so, I find that I am always blessed.

Prayer is the way in which we communicate with God, and he wants to get to know us better. Communication opens up the channel of knowing the person we are in relationship with better. Communication and praying often will help us to deepen our relationship with God. God wants us to pray.

"Rejoice always, pray without ceasing, give thanks in all circumstances; for this is the will of God in Christ Jesus for you."[43]

Fasting: Although this is not a book on fasting, I must give it a brief mention because prayer and fasting go together. Some prayers have to be accompanied by fasting. Jesus made his clear, *"And he said unto them, this kind can come forth by nothing, but by prayer and fasting."*[44]

Fasting is abstaining from something, in most cases, food, for spiritual purposes. It is an act of denying the body or the flesh so that we can be more focused on God in prayer.

---

[43] 1 Thessalonians 5:16-18 English Standard Version (ESV)
[44] Mark 9:29 King James Version (KJV)

"David prayed to God for the baby. David fasted and went into his house and stayed there, lying on the ground all night."[45]

Fasting can help in getting guidance and revelations. *"They chose elders for each church, by praying and fasting for a certain time. These elders had trusted the Lord, so Paul and Barnabas put them in the Lord's care."*[46]

Fasting is also good for the general well-being of the body.

Jesus called for a time of fasting.

"Jesus answered, "The friends of the bridegroom are not sad while he is with them. But the time will come when the bridegroom will be taken from them, and then they will fast.[47]

Jesus placed fasting, prayer and financial giving on the same level.[48]

Paul suggests we need to give ourselves to prayer and fasting.

---

[45] 2 Samuel 12:16 New Century Version (NCV)
[46] Acts 14:23 New Century Version (NCV), see also Acts 13:2.
[47] Matthew 9:15 New Century Version (NCV)
[48] See, Matthew 6:1-18

"Do not refuse to give your bodies to each other, unless you both agree to stay away from sexual relations for a time so you can give your time to prayer. Then come together again so Satan cannot tempt you because of a lack of self-control."[49]

There are different kinds of fasting such as:

Absolute fast, "Go and get all the Jewish people in Susa together. For my sake, fast; do not eat or drink for three days, night and day. I and my servant girls will also fast. Then I will go to the king, even though it is against the law, and if I die, I die."[50]

Partial fast, "Daniel said to the guard, "Please give us this test for ten days: Don't give us anything but vegetables to eat and water to drink."[51]

Normal fast. One can have just water, no other drinks or food.

Here are a few examples of fasting in the bible.

Moses (Exodus 34:28)

---

[49] 1 Corinthians 7:5 New Century Version (NCV)
[50] Esther 4:16 New Century Version (NCV)
[51] Daniel 1:12 New Century Version (NCV)

David (2 Samuel 12:16)

Nehemiah (Nehemiah 1:4)

Esther (Esther 4:16)

Daniel (Daniel 1:2)

Anna (Luke2:37)

Paul (Acts 14:23)

Jesus (Matthew 4:1-2)

The body of Christ, corporate (Acts 13:2)

CHAPTER TWO
How of prayers, Using Templates

"Lord, teach us to pray as John taught his followers."- Luke 11:1

THE DISCIPLES OF JESUS CHRIST WERE FACED WITH THE DIFFICULTY OF HOW TO PRAY. So they went to the Lord Jesus and said. *"Lord, teach us to pray as John taught his followers."*[52]

Without a doubt Jesus prayed a lot. Most if not all Jewish people learned how to pray as they grow up. Jesus' disciples asked him to teach them to pray.

"One day Jesus was praying in a certain place. When he finished, one of his disciples said to him, 'Lord, teach us to pray'".[53]

---

[52] Luke 11:1

I believe since these Jewish disciples already knew how to pray based on their cultural upbringing, they wanted to know how to pray like Jesus- taking it to another level where we receive that life-giving experience that comes not from just saying a memorized prayer, but from being in conversation with God.

They were saying 'Can you teach us to pray, being original, with passion, like we mean it?'

It is not a shameful thing not to know how to pray. If you do not know how to do a thing that it is important for you to be able to do, then seek the knowledge because it is a beautiful thing. Apostle Paul said,

> *"But before people can ask the Lord for help, they must believe in him; and before they can believe in him, they must hear about him; and for them to hear about the Lord, someone must tell them; and before someone can go and tell them, that person must be sent. It is written, "How beautiful is the person who comes to bring good news."*[54]

---

[53] Luke 11:1
[54] Romans 10:14-15 New Century Version (NCV)

When we are in a meaningful relationship we go out of our way to learn how to do things that will enhance the relationship so that it becomes significant.

An Arab proverbs says, *"There are four kinds of people, three of which are to be avoided and the fourth cultivated: those who don't know that they don't know; those who know that they don't know; those who don't know that they know; and those who know that they know"*[55]

The same proverb expressed in another way reads,
"Men are four:
He who knows not and knows not he knows not, he is a fool—shun him;
He who knows not and knows he knows not, he is simple—teach him;
He who knows and knows not he knows, he is asleep—wake him;
He who knows and knows he knows, he is wise—follow him !" [56]

---

[55] Anon. Rendering of the Arab Proverb
[56] Lady Burton—*Life of Sir Richard Burton*. Given as an Arabian Proverb. Another rendering in the *Spectator*, Aug. 11, 1894. P. 176. In Hesiod—*Works and Days*. 293. 7. Quoted by Aristotle—*Nic. Eth.* I. 4. Cicero—*Pro Cluent*. 31. Livy—*Works*. XXII. 29.

The disciples noted that John, the fore-runner of Jesus Christ taught his followers how to pray and wanted Jesus to do the same for them. Jesus taught his followers the topics of prayer that they should bring before God. Jesus taught the best-known prayer in the world, the Lord's Prayer.

> *"Jesus said to them, "When you pray, say: 'Father, may your name always be kept holy. May your kingdom come. Give us the food we need for each day. Forgive us for our sins, because we forgive everyone who has done wrong to us. And do not cause us to be tempted.'"*[57]

If you want to reinvigorate your conversations and be original, personal and passionate with God, I encourage you to make the Lord's Prayer your own. Take each of the seven phrases, putting the idea in your own words and then personalizing it. Pray it in your own way, using your own words and expressions.

This is the prayer that comes to be known as the Lord's Prayer.

---

[57] Luke 11:2-4

Our Father, which art in heaven,
Hallowed be thy Name.
Thy Kingdom come.
Thy will be done in earth,
as it is in heaven.
Give us this day our daily bread.
And forgive us our trespasses,
as we forgive them that trespass against us.
And lead us not into temptation,
but deliver us from evil.
For thine is the kingdom,
the power, and the glory,
For ever and ever. Amen.[58]

    The **Lord's Prayer** is a template of prayer. It is a pattern we can use for processing our prayer. It is a guide on how we can pray. It is comprised of us thanking and giving praise and worship to God for whom God is. Then we pray for God's will to be done. We ask for our needs and for forgiveness of our sins as we practice forgiveness in our lives. Finally we ask for God's protection and deliverance from all manner of evil and close with adoration to God.

---

[58] Taken from the Anglican Book of Common Prayer, 1662

There are numerous other templates or formulas we can use to help us in developing a healthy life of prayer.

We can start by what I call **"noting"** or **"underlining"** when we read. This is just developing a practice of noting with a letter 'P' (Pray) or just underline portions of our readings for us to come back to and pray about as we read.

For example I can note or underline Ephesians 1:15-23 in my reading and use it as a prayer template.

> *"That is why since I heard about your faith in the Lord Jesus and your love for all God's people, I have not stopped giving thanks to God for you. I always remember you in my prayers, asking the God of our Lord Jesus Christ, the glorious Father, to give you a spirit of wisdom and revelation so that you will know him better. I pray also that you will have greater understanding in your heart so you will know the hope to which he has called us and that you will know how rich and glorious are the blessings God has promised his holy people. And you will know that God's power is very great for us who believe. That power is the same as the great strength God used to raise Christ from the dead and put him at his right side in the heavenly world. God has put Christ over all rulers, authorities, powers, and kings, not only in this world but also in the next. God*

put everything under his power and made him the head over everything for the church, ^which^ is Christ's body. The church is filled with Christ, and Christ fills everything in every way".[59]

We can actually use the **Scriptures** as a prayer template.

For example Psalm 23.

*"The LORD is my shepherd; I have everything I need.
He lets me rest in green pastures. He leads me to calm water.
He gives me new strength. He leads me on paths that are right for the good of his name.*

Even if I walk through a very dark valley, I will not be afraid, because you are with me. Your rod and your shepherd's staff comfort me.

You prepare a meal for me in front of my enemies. You pour oil of blessing on my head; you fill my cup to overflowing. Surely your goodness and love will be with me all my life, and I will live in the house of the LORD forever.[60]

---

[59] Ephesians 1:15-23 New Century Version (NCV)
[60] Psalm 23 New Century Version (NCV)

In my own words I can pray, "Lord I thank you for being in my life. You are my God, my provider; you are the lifter of my head. You give me everything I need and so I lack nothing. Thank you for giving me rest, for giving me peace and for making this the place I need to be right now. Thank you for giving me comfort and for giving me strength. Lord, I am feeling weak right now, please renew my strength. Give me your joy because I am strengthened by it.[61]

God I need your directions, please lead me and my family. We need to make some decisions, please lead us on the right path. As we go through this difficult time in our lives be with us and comfort us, please provide a way for us.

Bless us Lord even in the midst of our trials when all hope seems to be gone. Please show up on our behalf and bless us to overflowing so that we will have extra and be a blessings to others in need. Keep us steady in your house, let us stay and abide under your shadows God. …"[62]

Another example of template we can use in prayer is some **memorable phrase or sentence**: E.g. "God is in

---

[61] Nehemiah 8:10, Psalm 28:7
[62] See Psalms 91.

charge, despite all appearances to the contrary. This is what we believe, this is what we have seen, and this is what we have to share with our world."

We can use this to jumpstart our prayers. For example, one can pray, 'God you are in charge of my job, you are in charge of my home, you are in charge of my spouse, and you are in charge of my family…. God take charge in spite of the present difficulties we are experiencing in our finances.

God, you are in charge of our provisions. You have always been in charge. When we were young, and now we that we are old, we have never seen good people left helpless or their children begging for food.[63] You are in charge God, we thank you as you meet our present and our future needs…'

The **ACTSS Template** is an acronym which provides a template for prayer for many people. The steps are **A**doration, **C**onfession, **T**hanksgiving, **S**upplication, and **S**ubmission.

"Do not be anxious about anything, but in every situation, by prayer and petition, with thanksgiving, present your requests to God." Philippians 4:6.

---

[63] Psalm 37:25 New Century Version (NCV)

Adoration is worship or veneration we give to God to express our deep love and respect.

Confession is a statement that acknowledges some personal facts that we would prefer to keep to ourselves especially after having done something wrong, whether on purpose or not. This is the confessions of our sins to God. You may argue that you do not sin, but, *"If we say we have no sin, we are fooling ourselves, and the truth is not in us."*[64]

In **Thanksgiving**, we are expressing our appreciation for God's goodness, for God's mercies and grace for us. *Give thanks to the LORD because he is good.* His love continues forever.[65]

Supplication is the act of asking or begging for something earnestly or humbly. This is the time to ask God.

"Ask, and God will give to you. Search, and you will find. Knock, and the door will open for you. Yes, everyone who asks will receive. Everyone who searches will find. And everyone who knocks will have the door opened." [66]

Submission is yielding to God's authority in prayer. It is accepting God's will and thanking God for God's response to

---

[64] 1 John 1:8 New Century Version (NCV)
[65] See Psalm 136
[66] Matthew 7:7-8 New Century Version (NCV)

our prayers, in other words, we leave everything in God's hands and trust God for the best outcome.

The BLESS Template is also an acronym. The prayers are focused on people:

Body - God to bless their physical and material needs, health and well-being.

Labor - God to bless their work, jobs, careers, finance and economic interest.

Emotions - God to bless their emotions, mental health and personal relationships.

Social - God to bless their social interactions with friends, relatives, associates, and neighbors, teachers, leaders and the political situations, social justice etc..

Spiritual - God to bless their spiritual life, the church and her leaders.

We can also use the **Published Prayer Template.** Here we make use of published prayer as a template. E.g. find a way to pray the announcements. We can find things to pray for and about just by paying attention to the on goings in our environment. News on our various channels of social media gives endless items and situations in need of our prayers.

As a young Christian I was taught in the disciples' class to use the **Hand Template.** This is simply assigning some specific prayer points to our thumb and fingers.

After prayers of thanksgiving and confessions, we follow this order in praying:

Thumb - prayers for our beloved, friends, family, and close associates.

Index/**P**ointer finger – prayers for leaders, teachers and people in places of leadership and authority

Middle finger – prayers for equity and general needs that will bring balance

Ring finger – prayers for the weak and vulnerable, the sick, the poor

Pinky finger -   personal prayers for self

Picture / Art work Template; the focus here is to use pictures as our prayer template. Henri J. M. Nouwen referred to this as praying with icons.[67] He suggested praying with the following icons. 1.) The icon of the Holy Spirit: Living in the house of love. 2.) The icon of the Virgin of Vladimir:

---

[67] See Henri J.M. Nouwen, *Behold the Beauty of the Lord; Praying with Icons,* Ave Maria Press, Notre dame, Indiana, 1987.

Belonging to God. 3.) The icon of the savior of Zvenigorod: Seeing Christ. 4.) The icon of the Descent of the Holy Spirit: Liberating the Word. As we look at the picture(s), we see something divine and use that to guide our prayers.

Prayer of Jabez Template; the notion is similar to using the Lord's Prayer as a template.

> *"⁹Jabez was more honorable than his brothers. His mother had named him Jabez, saying, "I gave birth to him in pain." Jabez cried out to the God of Israel, "Oh that you would bless me and enlarge my territory! Let your hand be with me, and keep me from harm so that I will be free from pain." And God granted his request."*[68]

We see key areas of focus as God's blessings, enlargement or increase, God's presence, God's protection and peace.

Quaker Prayer Template presumes that God longs to spend time with us if we just quiet down and listen. Here we go to God with no agenda. We are just quiet in God's presence.

---

[68] 1 Chronicles 4:9-10 New International Version (NIV)

If The Holy Spirit drops something in our heart to pray about then we pray, if not we are just there listening to whatever God wants to tell us.

God says, "Be still and know that I am God..."[69]

This is by no means the end of our templates, God keeps adding to the list. I will discuss imaginative prayers and flesh out specific imaginative prayers templates in the next chapter.

---

[69] Psalm 46:10 New Century Version (NCV)

CHAPTER THREE
Imaginative Prayers

"That the God of our Lord Jesus Christ, the Father of glory, may give unto you the spirit of wisdom and revelation in the knowledge of him: The eyes of your understanding being enlightened; that ye may know what is the hope of his calling, and what the riches of the glory of his inheritance in the saints," -Ephesians 1:17-18

MANY CHRISTIANS ARE USED TO PRAYING WRITTEN PRAYERS OR PRAYING EXTEMPORE. We tend to have some prayer lines that we have become accustomed to. We recite some prayers; we say certain prayers at certain occasions, e.g. giving thanks at meal time. But prayer can be more.

Some of us have probably heard of a prayer techniques popularized by St. Ignatius of Loyola, the founder of the Jesuits, called "imaginative prayer," or "Ignatian contemplation," or, "composition of place." This approach had been around in various forms before Ignatius used it in his classic sixteenth-century text, *The Spiritual Exercises.*

The Ignatian prayer places great emphasis on the power of the imagination to deepen our relationship with God. One of the principal forms of prayer in the Spiritual Exercises is imaginative reflection on scenes from the Gospels.

In imaginative prayer we attempt to place ourselves in a biblical scene by using our imagination. Then you reflect on what God has revealed to you through your prayer. This kind of imaginative prayer seeks the truth of the heart rather than the truth of facts.

Here is an example with Mark's account of the healing of the paralyzed man (Mark 2:1-12). In this marvelous story, the man's friends cut a hole in the roof of a house in which Jesus is preaching. Then they lower their friend down, in the hope that Jesus will heal him.

You start by praying for God's presence, then, you read the passage and use your imagination to slowly set the scene; as St. Ignatius would say, you "compose the place" in your mind. You ask yourself: *Who am I in this gospel story?* Are you part of the excited crowd in attendance to see Jesus? Are you one of the man's friends who have climbed onto the roof and had the hard and dangerous job of getting their friend to Jesus by any means necessary? Are you the owner of the house, whose roof is being torn apart? Are you the paralyzed man?

Next: *What do I see?* You might imagine what the house looks like, along with the expression on Jesus' face, or the looks of the people in the crowd. Your imagination continues with focusing on what do you hear? What do you hear from the crowd? What do you hear from Jesus?

What do I hear? The gospel says that there were a lot of people in the house: were there confusing, riotous, or calm sounds?

You imagine *the smell*. Was it nice or foul? Were people sweating? Etc. Were there smells coming from the house itself? Or were there smells from domestic animals?

In these ways you use your imagination and your senses to place yourself within the scene. Then you let the gospel story unfold, as if you were watching a movie playing out.

You suddenly become fully engaged in the event and you are able to locate yourself and relate fully with a character in the story. You connect emotionally and find yourself praying for yourself in that character.

For example, you might find yourself watching the paralyzed man and feeling a deep hurt or illness, thinking, "I need some healing in my life!" Or you may connect with Jesus as a preacher and begin to feel a sense of commitment and urgency to do the work of ministry.

Imaginative prayer involves trusting that God is at work through your imagination and through whatever emotions or insights you may experience. Sometimes it may be difficult to do imaginative prayer, but God is always at work. Spiritual transformation is taking place at a deep level, even if you can't see it. Spending time with God always changes us.

Jesus constantly used the imagination of his listeners to teach and transform them. For example Jesus invited his listeners to be a widow searching for her lost coin. Jesus used the prodigal son returning home to beg for a job as a servant. Jesus brought in the lot of imaginations in the story of the Good Samaritan. Jesus always helps the listeners become involved in the story.

An imaginative prayer invites us to become a part of the gospel story being played out in our own lives. It helps us to remain true to the Biblical reading, and actively experience it.

I am proposing a different type or approach to our imaginative prayer in the form of developing an imaginative template with which we can pray.

God wants us to use our imaginations. Our imaginations will help us to articulate our argument. This is because God want us to have a robust discussion with him in our prayers.

> *"Produce your cause, saith the Lord; bring forth your strong reasons, saith the King of Jacob."*[70] God creates out of nothing. *"…This is true before God, the God Abraham believed, the God who gives life to the dead and who creates something out of nothing."*[71]

It takes superior imagination to be able to reason. Imagination is the bed-rock for sophisticated arguments. We need imaginations as building blocks to help us marshal out our prayers in a thoughtful manner. It takes imagination to pray in order to withstand the wiles of the devil.

> *"The weapons of our warfare are not physical [weapons of flesh and blood]. Our weapons are divinely powerful for the destruction of fortresses. We are destroying sophisticated arguments and every exalted and proud thing that sets itself up against the [true] knowledge of God, and we are taking every thought and purpose captive to the obedience of Christ, being ready to punish every act of disobedience, when your own obedience [as a church] is complete."*[72]

---

[70] Isaiah 41:21(KJV)
[71] Romans 4:17 New Century Version (NCV)
[72] 2 Corinthians 10:4-6 Amplified Bible (AMP)

It takes imagination to bring out our faith to call those things which are not as though they are. *"(as it is written, "I have made you a father of many nations") in the presence of Him whom he believed—God, who gives life to the dead and calls those things which do not exist as though they did;"*[73]

Think of the imagination as building blocks to be used in abstract thinking. In order to make it easy for us to understand, we shall always start from the known and go to the unknown. We will, like Jesus, proceed from the familiar to the unfamiliar.

This imagination is similar to what C. Wright Mills, called the 'Sociological imaginations'. It involves something called *making the familiar strange*. It is similar to putting on a new pair of glasses - in this case with sociological lenses - and seeing our society and the everyday behaviors and interactions we usually take for granted in a different way.

Developing the ability to pray using our imagination not only helps us to order and articulate our prayers, it helps us to be able to put things in perspectives that are real and

---

[73] Romans 4:17 New King James Version (NKJV)

meaningful to us. This imaginative perspective approach makes our prayer become deep and exciting at the same time.

By perspective, I am referring to the state of one's ideas, the facts known to one, etc., in having a meaningful interrelationship: or a mental view or prospect.[74]

Let us streamline this template by condensing it into three parts, for now. Like any theory, more shall be revealed with time.[75]

These three are:

1.) Structural Prayer Template.

2.) Interactive Prayer Template.

3.) Warfare Prayer Template.

---

[74] http://www.dictionary.com/browse/perspective

[75] "But as it is written in the Scriptures: "No one has ever seen this, and no one has ever heard about it.
No one has ever imagined what God has prepared for those who love him." 1 Corinthians 2:9 New Century Version (NCV)

CHAPTER FOUR
Imaginative Structural Prayer Template

"For precept must be upon precept, precept upon precept; line upon line, line upon line; here a little, and there a little:" Isaiah 28:10

THIS TEMPLATE FOCUSES OUR IMAGINATION ON THE STRUCTURES THAT MAKE OUR LIFE POSSIBLE AND RELATIVELY STABLE. What happens here is we focus on a structure that we are familiar and comfortable with, and we systematically use the various functional parts of the structure to order our prayers. It is like building a structure from the ground up as we pray by paying attention to the various parts that make up the whole.

Each part of the structure is important because it has a function. The parts come together to make the whole. For example, as a part of the human body, "The eye cannot say to the hand, "I don't need you!" And the head cannot say to the foot, "I don't need you!"[76]

Once we start the prayers, with our imaginations starting from one part, we continue adding parts until we get to the whole.

> *"Because you have these blessings, do your best to add these things to your lives: to your faith, add goodness; and to your goodness, add knowledge; and to your knowledge, add self-control; and to your self-control, add patience; and to your patience, add service for God;"*[77]

Here is an example of how to use the imaginative structural prayer template. In this example I will illustrate with the structure of a house.

---

[76] 1 Corinthians 12:21 New Century Version (NCV)
[77] 2 Peter 1:5-6 New Century Version (NCV)

We begin to imagine the structure of a house and use the imagination of that structure to pray. Most houses for example would have a foundation (usually not in plain view), the walls, windows, rooms etc., (that we see) and, finally, the ceiling and roof as the covering. We start to pray about foundational things in our lives that need to be deep and strong.

Then, we move on to the things that we see, things that can be changed and moved around.

Finally, we pray for the things above us, that gives cover and protection.

We can allow our imaginations to run as we pray for the different parts of the structure.

If we are using a car as the structure in our prayer template for example; we may imagine the car being dirty as a result of accumulated filth and dirt over time and imagine us cleaning out the car and praying for God to cleanse us.

Such an imagination will bring this prayer of David home to us.

"Create in me a pure heart, God, and make my spirit right again."[78]

From our imaginations of the structures we are familiar with, we will be able to relate such to whatever we are going through in our lives.

This can help us shape and direct our prayers. By imagining the structure of a car in our prayers, we may observe the deflated tire which, if not fixed, grounds the whole vehicle.

Such imaginings can be translated to similar minor or major issues in our lives that need prayer because they hinder us from operating at full capacity as God intended.

The minor issue for example may have a huge effect. Be careful! *"Just a little yeast makes the whole batch of dough rise."*[79] God's plan for us, just like our plans for our vehicles, is to operate at full capacity.[80]

---

[78] Psalm 51:10 New Century Version (NCV)
[79] Galatians 5:9 New Century Version (NCV)
[80] I say this because I know what I am planning for you," says the LORD. "I have good plans for you, not plans to hurt you. I will give you hope and a good future. Jeremiah 29:11 New Century Version (NCV).

CHAPTER FIVE
Imaginative Interactive Prayer Template

"Try to live in peace with all people, and try to live free from sin. Anyone whose life is not holy will never see the Lord." - Hebrews 12:14

"Do your best to live in peace with everyone." -Romans 12:18

"First, I tell you to pray for all people, asking God for what they need and being thankful to him." -1 Timothy 2:1

T HIS TEMPLATE FOCUSES OUR IMAGINATION ON THE PROCESS OF SOCIAL INTERACTION THAT BRINGS MEANING TO OUR LIVES. Our lives consist of relationships. We are not created to be alone.[81]

We have heard the phrase, "No man (I add, woman) is an island." Human beings do not thrive when isolated from others.

Here is the full Quotation by John Donne:

"All mankind is of one author, and is one volume; when one man dies, one chapter is not torn out of the book, but translated into a better language; and every chapter must be so translated...As therefore the bell that rings to a sermon, calls not upon the preacher only, but upon the congregation to come: so this bell calls us all: but how much more me, who am brought so near the door by this sickness....No man is an island, entire of itself...any man's death diminishes me, because I am involved in mankind; and therefore never send to know for whom the bell tolls; it tolls for thee."[82]

---

[81] Then the LORD God said, "It is not good for the man to be alone. I will make a helper who is right for him." Genesis 2:18 New Century Version (NCV)

[82] This is a quotation from John Donne (1572-1631). Donne was a Christian but this concept is shared by other religions, principally

IMAGINATIVE PRAYER TEMPLATES

I believe we are not created to be alone. We thrive in relationships, albeit in good relationships. We are always in a relationship, either with a real or perceived other, which may be physically present or otherwise.

Jesus makes this obvious while warning his followers about the time of separation. Even at that time, Jesus was not alone.

> *"Listen to me; a time is coming when you will be scattered, each to your own home. That time is now here. You will leave me alone, but I am never really alone, because the Father is with me."*[83]

Praying, using Imaginative Interactive Prayer Templates entails using our imaginations to see our relationships and then pray about them. For example, in a family setting, we can imagine the web of relationships around us to focus our prayers.

We see in our minds the people in our family and begin to pray for - parent(s), children, siblings, grandparents, grandchildren, aunts, uncles, nieces, nephews, cousins, husband, wife, in-laws, partners, fiancé, step parents, ex, etc.

Buddhism. It appears in *Devotions upon emergent occasions and several steps in my sickness - Meditation XVII*, 1624

[83] John 16:32 New Century Version (NCV)

The child might want to thank God for the parent's love and attention while at the same time ask God for patience to deal with a sibling with whom they do not get along well.

Imaginative Interactive Prayer Templates will help us focus on the kind of relationships that is godly and help us thrive.

We sincerely focus the beam of imagination on ourselves in our relationships, we look at the things we are or are not doing to make the relationships better and then make our imaginations the focus of our prayers.

Imaginative Interactive Prayer is inward looking.

"Why do you look at the speck of sawdust in your brother's eye and pay no attention to the plank in your own eye? How can you say to your brother, 'Let me take the speck out of your eye,' when all the time there is a plank in your own eye? You hypocrite, first take the plank out of your own eye, and then you will see clearly to remove the speck from your brother's eye.[84]

Imaginative Interactive Prayer brings healing.

---

[84] Matthew 7:3-5 New International Version (NIV)

James advised, *"Confess your sins to each other and pray for each other so God can heal you. When a believing person prays, great things happen."*[85]

---

[85] James 5:16 New Century Version (NCV)

CHAPTER SIX

Imaginative Warfare Prayer Template

"Be alert and of sober mind. Your enemy the devil prowls around like a roaring lion looking for someone to devour." -1 Peter 5:8

"...lest Satan should take advantage of us; for we are not ignorant of his devices."
-2 Corinthians 2:11

"Indeed, we live as human beings, but we do not wage war according to human standards; for the weapons of our warfare are not merely human, but they have divine power to destroy strongholds. We destroy

arguments and every proud obstacle raised up against the knowledge of God, and we take every thought captive to obey Christ. We are ready to punish every disobedience when your obedience is complete." -2 Corinthians 10:3-6

IMAGINATIVE WARFARE PRAYER TEMPLATE FOCUSES ON THE POINTS OF CONFLICT IN OUR LIVES. Using this templates we begin to direct our attention to contentious and conflicting issues affecting us.

We begin to imagine the areas of tension and direct specific prayers to such.

For example, through our imaginations we may be able to observe the struggle for power, dominance and control among people that we work with or even within our family and thus direct our prayers appropriately.

We may see clearly through our imaginations the role of coercion and power around us and the effect on order. With the power of the Holy Spirit we will be able to direct our prayers to the source of any problem.

Using the warfare prayer template helps us to stay alert and be vigilant and not take things for granted. We escape being blind-sided.

"While people are saying, 'We have peace and we are safe,' they will be destroyed quickly. It is like pains that come quickly to a woman having a baby. Those people will not escape."[86]

This template will help us to reflect on conflict.

"Finally, all of you should be in agreement, understanding each other, loving each other as family, being kind and humble. Do not do wrong to repay a wrong, and do not insult to repay an insult. But repay with a blessing, because you yourselves were called to do this so that you might receive a blessing. The Scripture says, "A person must do these things to enjoy life and have many happy days. He must not say evil things, and he must not tell lies. He must stop doing evil and do good. He must look for peace and work for it."[87]

---

[86] 1 Thessalonians 5:3 New Century Version (NCV)
[87] 1 Peter 3:8-11 New Century Version (NCV)

CHAPTER SEVEN

Scriptural References on Prayer

"One day Jesus told his disciples a story to show that they should always pray and never give up."- 2 Corinthians 10:3-6

Please read and take time to study them, especially by reading and studying verses before and after these scriptures for a better understanding of their content.

Take your time to read slowly over and over again and, please allow the Holy Spirit to interpret them to you.

"But please listen to my prayer and my request, because I am your servant. LORD my God, hear this prayer your servant prays to you today. ²⁹ Night and day please watch over this Temple where you have said, 'I will be worshiped there.' Hear the prayer I pray facing this Temple." 1 Kings 8:28-29

"Depend on the LORD and his strength; always go to him for help." 1 Chronicles 16:11

"Hear my prayers and the prayers of your people Israel when we pray facing this place. Hear from your home in heaven, and when you hear, forgive us." 2 Chronicles 6:21

*"Then if my people, who are called by my name, will humble themselves, if they will pray and seek me and stop their evil ways, I will hear them from heaven. I will forgive their sin, and I will heal their land. "*2 Chronicles 7:14

"You will pray to him, and he will hear you, and you will keep your promises to him." Job 22:27

"Then you will call my name. You will come to me and pray to me, and I will listen to you." Jeremiah 29:12

"Answer me when I pray to you, my God who does what is right. Make things easier for me when I am in trouble. Have mercy on me and hear my prayer." Psalm 4:1

"I call to you, God, and you answer me. Listen to me now, and hear what I say." Psalm 17:6

"God, listen to my complaint. I am afraid of my enemies; protect my life from them." Psalms 64:1

"Lord God All-Powerful, hear my prayer; God of Jacob, listen to me. Selah" Psalms 84:8

"He will answer the prayers of the needy; he will not reject their prayers." Psalm 102:17

"In their misery they cried out to the Lord, and he saved them from their troubles. He stilled the storm and calmed the waves. They were happy that it was quiet, and God guided them to the port they wanted." Psalm 107:28-30

"Let my prayer be like incense placed before you, and my praise like the evening sacrifice." Psalm 141:2

"The LORD is close to everyone who prays to him, to all who truly pray to him." Psalm 145:18

"The LORD hates the sacrifice that the wicked offer, but he likes the prayers of honest people." Proverbs 15:8

"The LORD does not listen to the wicked, but he hears the prayers of those who do right." Proverbs 15:29

" "Now, our God, hear the prayers of your servant. Listen to my prayer for help, and for your sake do good things for your holy place that is in ruins." Daniel 9:17

"When my life had almost gone, I remembered the LORD. I prayed to you, and you heard my prayers in your Holy Temple." Jonah 2:7

"But I say to you, love your enemies. Pray for those who hurt you." Matthew 5:44

"And when you pray, don't be like those people who don't know God. They continue saying things that mean nothing, thinking that God will hear them because of their many words." Matthew 6:7

"So when you pray, you should pray like this: 'Our Father in heaven, may your name always be kept holy. May your kingdom come and what you want be done, here on earth as it is in heaven. Give us the food we need for each day. Forgive us for our sins, just as we have forgiven those who sinned against us. And do not cause us to be tempted, but save us from the Evil One.' The kingdom, the power, and the glory are yours forever. Amen."
Matthew 6:9-13

"Ask, and God will give to you. Search, and you will find. Knock, and the door will open for you." Matthew 7:7

"Even though you are bad, you know how to give good gifts to your children. How much more your heavenly Father will give good things to those who ask him!" Matthew 7:11

"If you believe, you will get anything you ask for in prayer."
Matthew 21:22

"How terrible for you, teachers of the law and Pharisees. You are hypocrites. You take away widows' houses, and you say long prayers so that people will notice you. So you will have a worse punishment." Matthew 23:14

"Stay awake and pray for strength against temptation. The spirit wants to do what is right, but the body is weak." Matthew 26:41

"Jesus answered, "That kind of spirit can only be forced out by prayer." Mark 9:29

"So I tell you to believe that you have received the things you ask for in prayer, and God will give them to you." Mark 11:24

"At that time Jesus went off to a mountain to pray, and he spent the night praying to God." Luke 6:12

"Then Jesus used this story to teach his followers that they should always pray and never lose hope. " Luke 18:1

"And if you ask for anything in my name, I will do it for you so that the Father's glory will be shown through the Son. [14] If you ask me for anything in my name, I will do it." John 14:13-14

"I am not asking you to take them out of the world but to keep them safe from the Evil One." John 17:15

"So Peter was kept in jail, but the church prayed earnestly to God for him." Acts 12:5

"Also, the Spirit helps us with our weakness. We do not know how to pray as we should. But the Spirit himself speaks to God for us, even begs God for us with deep feelings that words cannot explain." Romans 8:26

"Brothers and sisters, the thing I want most is for all the Jews to be saved. That is my prayer to God." Romans 10:1

"Be joyful because you have hope. Be patient when trouble comes, and pray at all times." Romans 12:12

"Peter sent everyone out of the room and kneeled and prayed. Then He turned to the body and said, "Tabitha, stand up." She opened her eyes, and when she saw Peter, she sat up." Acts 9:40

"I pray also that you will have greater understanding in your heart so you will know the hope to which he has called us and that you will know how rich and glorious are the blessings God has promised his holy people." Ephesians 1:18

"Pray in the Spirit at all times with all kinds of prayers, asking for everything you need. To do this you must always be ready and never give up. Always pray for all God's people."
Ephesians 6:18

"Do not worry about anything, but pray and ask God for everything you need, always giving thanks. And God's peace, which is so great we cannot understand it, will keep your hearts and minds in Christ Jesus." Philippians 4:6-7

"Continue praying, keeping alert, and always thanking God." Colossians 4:2

"Pray continually," 1 Thessalonians 5:17

"First, I tell you to pray for all people, asking God for what they need and being thankful to him. Pray for rulers and for all who have authority so that we can have quiet and peaceful lives full of worship and respect for God." 1 Timothy 2:1-2

"So, I want the men everywhere to pray, lifting up their hands in a holy manner, without anger and arguments." 1 Timothy 2:8

"Since we have a great high priest, Jesus the Son of God, who has gone into heaven, let us hold on to the faith we have." Hebrews 4:14

"But if any of you needs wisdom, you should ask God for it. He is generous to everyone and will give you wisdom without criticizing you. But when you ask God, you must believe and not doubt. Anyone who doubts is like a wave in the sea, blown up and down by the wind. Such doubters are thinking two different things at the same time, and they cannot decide about anything they do. They should not think they will receive anything from the Lord." James 1:5-8

"Or when you ask, you do not receive because the reason you ask is wrong. You want things so you can use them for your own pleasures." James 4:3

"Anyone who is having troubles should pray. Anyone who is happy should sing praises." James 5:13

*"Anyone who is sick should call the church's elders. They should pray for and pour oil on the person in the name of the Lord. And the prayer that is said with faith will make the sick person well; the Lord will heal that person. And if the person has sinned, the

sins will be forgiven. Confess your sins to each other and pray for each other so God can heal you. When a believing person prays, great things happen." James 5:14-16

*"But if we confess our sins, he will forgive our sins, because we can trust God to do what is right. He will cleanse us from all the wrongs we have done. "*1 John 1:9

"And this is the boldness we have in God's presence: that if we ask God for anything that agrees with what he wants, he hears us. If we know he hears us every time we ask him, we know we have what we ask from him.

If anyone sees a brother or sister sinning (sin that does not lead to eternal death), that person should pray, and God will give the sinner life. I am talking about people whose sin does not lead to eternal death. There is sin that leads to death. I do not mean that a person should pray about that sin."

1 John 5:14-16

IMAGINATIVE PRAYER TEMPLATES

APPENDIX I
222 Prayers of the Bible[88]

THE FOLLOWING LIST OF BIBLE PRAYERS IS FROM THE DAKE'S ANNOTATED REFERENCE BIBLE, KING JAMES VERSION (USED BY PERMISSION).

Dake found one hundred and seventy six prayers in the Old Testament and 46 in the New Testament. These include only actual worded prayers, not references to prayer. All statements such as "he prayed, he entreated the Lord, he called

---

[88] https://www.hopefaithprayer.com/prayernew/222-prayers-of-the-bible/

upon the name of the Lord," etc., are not prayers; they merely mention that certain people prayed.

Six Prayers in Genesis.

1. Abraham for an heir (Genesis 15:2-3). Answered because God had promised (Genesis 21:1-8).

2. Abraham for Ishmael to be his heir (Genesis 17:18). Unanswered because it was not in harmony with God's word and plan.

3. Abraham for Sodom to be spared if 10 persons were righteous (Genesis 18:23-32). Unanswered because 10 righteous persons were not found (Genesis 19:24).

4. Eliezer, steward of Abraham, for a bride for Isaac (Genesis 24:12-14). Answered because it was according to God's word (Genesis 12:1-3, 7; 13:15; 15:18; 17:7, 19; 21:12).

5. Jacob for a blessing (Genesis 28:20-22). Answered because of God's plan for him (Genesis 32:1-33:17).

6. Jacob for deliverance from Esau (Genesis 32:9-12). Answered because of God's word and plan for him (Genesis 25:19-23; 26:3; 27:28-29; 28:3-4, 13-15; 32:9).

References to prayer, entreating the Lord, calling on the name of the Lord, and groaning and being afflicted (Genesis 12:7-8; 13:4; 16:11; 20:17-18; 25:21-23).

Four Prayers in Exodus:

7. Moses for Aaron to go with him (Exodus 4:13). Answered because God wanted to please Moses (Exodus 4:14-17).

8. Moses in complaint to God for not delivering Israel (Exodus 5:22-23). Answered because of God's word (Exodus 3:8, 12, 17-22).

9. Moses for forgiveness for Israel (39 words; Exodus 32:31-32). Answered because of atonement and intercession (Exodus 32:11-14, 30-35) and because of God's word (Exodus 33:1-6, 12-14).

10. Moses for God's presence to go with Israel to Canaan (Exodus 33:12-13, 15-16). Answered because of God's word (Exodus 33:12-14) and His grace (Exodus 33:17).

References to groaning, sighing, crying, and entreating the Lord (Exodus 2:11, 23-25; 3:7, 9; 10:16).

Nine Prayers in Numbers

11. Aaron for the blessing of God upon the people (Numbers 6:24-26). Answered because of God's promise (Numbers 6:27).

12. Moses for God to bless on the journey (Numbers 10:35-36). Answered when Israel lived free from sin, but unanswered when they sinned, which was according to God's word (Ex 32:32-33).

13. Moses in complaining to God because the burden was too heavy (Numbers 11:10-15). Answered because of God's words (Numbers 11:16-20, 25-30).

14. Moses for God to show him what to do to give the people flesh (Numbers 11:21-22). Answered because of God's word (Numbers 11:21) and to show His power (Numbers 11:23).

15. Moses for the healing of Miriam (Numbers 12:13). Answered because of God's love for Moses (Numbers 12:14-16).

16. Moses for God to spare Israel and uphold His own honor (Numbers14:13-19). Answered because of Moses' prayer (Numbers 14:20).

17. Moses for judgment on sin (Numbers 16:15). Answered because of sin (Numbers16:23-34).

18. Israel for forgiveness of sin (Numbers 21:7). Answered because of Moses' prayer and by type of Christ on the cross (Numbers 21:7-9; 3:14-16).

19. Moses for a new leader of Israel (Numbers 27:16-17). Answered because of God's plan for Israel (Numbers 27:18-23).

References to prayer (Numbers 11:2; 21:7).

Two Prayers in Deuteronomy

20. Moses asking to go over into Canaan (Deuteronomy 3:24-25). Unanswered because of sin (Deuteronomy 3:26; Numbers 20:12).

21. Moses for Israel to be spared (Deuteronomy 9:26-29). Answered because of intercession of Moses (Ex 32:11-14).

References to prayer (Deuteronomy 9:20,26), also what to pray for elders at murder trials (Deuteronomy 21:6-9) and what all Israel should pray after obedience to the law (Deuteronomy 26:5-15).

Two Prayers in Joshua

22. Joshua in complaint because God had not given victory (90 words; Joshua 7:7-9). Answered so sin could be put away (Joshua 7:10-15).

23. Joshua in the form of a command for the sun and moon to stand still (14 words; Joshua 10:12). Answered because of necessity for time to finish God's work (Joshua 10:13).

Nine Prayers in Judges

24. Israel for guidance (Judges 1:1). Answered because it was in harmony with the will of God for the nation (Judges 1:2).

25. Gideon for revelation and guidance (Judges 6:13, 15, 17-18, 22). Answered because of God's word and will for Israel (Judges 6:12, 14, 16, 20-21, 23).

26. Israel for deliverance and forgiveness of sins (Judges 10:10, 15). Answered because of God's plan for Israel (Judges 11:1-33).

27. Jephthah for victory (Judges 11:30-31). Answered because of God's plan for Israel (Judges 11:32).

28. Manoah for an angel to appear and give him directions (Judges 13:8, 11-12, 15, and 17). Answered because of God's plan for Israel (Judges 13:9, 11, 13, 16, 18).

29. Samson for one last victory (Judges 16:28). Answered because of his re-consecration to the Nazarite vows (Judges 13:4-5; 16:22).

30. Israel for guidance (Judges 20:23). Answered because of judgment on sin.

31. Israel for guidance (Judges 20:28). Answered because of judgment on sin.

32. Israel for revelation (Judges 21:3). No answer recorded.

Six Prayers in 1 Samuel

33. Hannah for a son (1 Samuel 1:11). Answered because of God's plan for Israel (1 Samuel 1:20-23) and promises to bless

IMAGINATIVE PRAYER TEMPLATES

with children upon obedience (Lev 26:3-13; Deuteronomy 28:1-14).

34. Hannah to express gratitude for answered prayer (1 Samuel 2:1-10). No request to answer.

35. Saul for guidance (1 Samuel 14:37). Unanswered because of sin (1 Samuel 13:1-14; 14:37).

36. David for guidance (1 Samuel 23:2). Answered because of God's plan (1 Samuel 23:2).

37. David for revelation (1 Samuel 23:10-12). Answered because of God's plan.

38. David for revelation (1 Samuel 30:8). Answered because of God's plan.

References to prayer (1 Samuel 7:9; 8:6; 12:18; 15:11; 28:6).

Four Prayers in 2 Samuel

39. David for revelation (2 Samuel 2:1). Answered because of God's plan.

40. David for revelation (2 Samuel 5:19). Answered because of God's plan (2 Samuel 5:19).

41. David for fulfillment of Davidic covenant (2 Samuel 7:18-29). Answered partially, and will be fulfilled in all eternity when Christ comes to reign (Isaiah 9:6-7; Luke 1:32-33; Acts 15:13-18; Revelation 11:15; 20:1-10).

42. David for forgiveness of sin (2 Samuel 24:10). Answered, but judgments fell (2 Samuel 24:11-25).

References to prayer (2 Samuel 5:23; 12:16; 15:7-8; 21:1).

Five Prayers in 1 Kings

43. Solomon for wisdom (1 Kings 3:6-9). Answered because it pleased God (1 Kings 3:10-14).

44. Solomon, prayer of dedication (1 Kings 8:23-53). Answered according to obedience of Israel.

45. Elijah for resurrection of boy (1 Kings 17:20-21). Answered because of faith in God (1 Kings 17:22-24; Hebrews 11:35).

46. Elijah for fire from heaven (1 Kings 18:36-37). Answered because of faith (1 Kings 18:38).

47. Elijah for death (1 Kings 19:4). Unanswered because it was contrary to God's plan which was to translate him and permit him to live bodily in heaven until time to come back to earth as

one of the two witnesses (2 Kings 2:9; Zechariah 4:11-14; Mal 4:5-6; Rev 11:3-11).

References to prayer (1 Kings 13:6; 18:42-43).

Three Prayers in 2 Kings

48. Elisha for his servant's eyes to be opened (2 Kings 6:17). Answered by faith.

49. Hezekiah for deliverance (2 Kings 19:15-19). Answered by faith (2 Kings 19:35).

50. Hezekiah for a longer life (he received 15 years more (2 Kings 20:3). Answered by faith (2 Kings 20:5-6).

Two Prayers in 1 Chronicles

51. Jabez for enlarged coast (1 Chronicles 4:10). Answered because of God's word to give Israel all the land (1 Chronicles 4:10; Gen 15:18-21).

52. David for Solomon and Israel (1 Chronicles 29:10-19). Answered partially, in the temporary obedience to God of Solomon and Israel.

References to prayer (1 Chronicles 5:20; 21:26; 23:30).

Two Prayers in 2 Chronicles

53. Asa for victory (2 Chronicles 14:11). Answered by faith (2 Chronicles 14:12-14).

54. Jehoshaphat for victory (2 Chronicles 20:6-12). Answered by faith (2 Chronicles 20:20-25).

References to prayer (2 Chronicles 15:13; 33:13).

Two Prayers in Ezra

55. Ezra-prayer of thanksgiving (Ezra 7:27-28).

56. Ezra for forgiveness and help (Ezra 9:5-15). Answered (Ezra 10:1-19).

References to prayer (Ezra 8:21-23).

Nine Prayers in Nehemiah

57. Nehemiah for confession of sins and help (256 words; Nehemiah 1:5-11).

58. Nehemiah for judgment (Nehemiah 4:1-6).

59. Nehemiah for help (Nehemiah 6:9).

60. Nehemiah for help (Nehemiah 6:14).

61. Israel-confession of sins (Nehemiah 9:5-38).

62. Nehemiah for blessing (Nehemiah 13:14).

63. Nehemiah for blessing (Nehemiah 13:22).

64. Nehemiah for judgment (Nehemiah 13:29).

65. Nehemiah for blessing (Nehemiah 1: 11).

References to prayer (Nehemiah 2:4; 4:9; 8:6).

Seven Prayers in Job

66. Job-prayer of thanksgiving and resignation (Job 1:20-22).

67. Job in complaint and for relief and forgiveness (Job 7:17-21). Answered (Job 42:10).

68. Job in complaint and for relief (Job 9:25-10:22). Answered (Job 42:10).

69. Job in complaint and for life and forgiveness (Job 14:13-22). Answered (Job 42:10).

70. Job for a fair trial (Job 23:3-5). Answered (Job 38-42).

71. Job, prayer of confession (Job 40:3-5)

72. Job, prayer of repentance (Job 42:1-6). Answered (Job 42:10).

Seventy-two Prayers in Psalms

73-123. David. In 50 prayer-psalms he made requests for various blessings, most of them being answered because of faith in God's promises (Psalms 3-7; 9; 12:1-13:6; 16:1-17:15; 19:1-20:9; 22; 25:1-31:24; 35:1-36:12; 38:1-41:13; 51; 54:1-61:8; 64; 69:1-70:5; 86; 108:1-109:31; 119; 124; 132; 139:1-144:15). The ones unanswered will be answered in due time because David even prayed about future events.

124-138. An unknown psalmist (perhaps David) prayed for many kinds of blessings, which were granted or will be granted (Psalms 10; 33; 43:1-44:26; 71; 85; 88; 102; 106; 118; 120; 123; 125; 129; 137).

139-143. Asaph made many requests to God (in 5 prayers) for various kinds of blessing which were granted or will be granted (Psalms 74; 79:1-80:19; 82:1-83:18).

144. Moses makes requests to God (Psalms 90).

145. Ethan made requests for God to remember the reproach of His servants (Psalms 89).

Thus, in 72 of the 150 psalms there are personal requests to God, making them definitely prayer-psalms. A few of the other 78 may also be considered such because of the general nature of the subject matter. Even in the listed prayer-psalms many subjects are more outstanding than the prayers.

Three Prayers in Isaiah

146. Isaiah for cleansing (Isaiah 6:5). Answered (Isaiah 6:6-7).

147. Hezekiah for deliverance (Isaiah 37:16-20). Answered (Isaiah 37:36).

148. Hezekiah for healing and length of days (Isaiah 38:3). Answered (Isaiah 38:5).

References to prayer (Isaiah 1:15; 7:11; 16:12; 26:16; 55:6-7). There are also prayers that Israel will make in the time of their restoration as a nation (Isaiah 12; 64).

Eleven Prayers in Jeremiah

149. Jeremiah, confession of inability to obey God (Jeremiah 1:6).

150. Jeremiah, accusing God (Jeremiah 4:10).

151. Jeremiah for judgment (Jeremiah 10:23-25). Answered (Daniel 5).

152. Jeremiah, questioning God (Jeremiah 12:1-4).

153. Jeremiah for help for Judah (Jeremiah 14:7-9).

154. Jeremiah for help for Judah (Jeremiah 14:20-22).

155. Jeremiah, judgment (Jeremiah 15:15-18).

156. Jeremiah for judgment (Jeremiah 17:13-18).

157. Jeremiah for judgment (Jeremiah 18:19-23).

158. Jeremiah for judgment (Jeremiah 20:7-12).

159. Jeremiah, concerning captivity of Judah (Jeremiah 32:17-25).

References to prayer (Jeremiah 7:16; 11:14; 14:11; 21:2; 29:7,12; 37:3; 42:2,4,20).

Four Prayers in Lamentations

160. Jeremiah for judgment (Lamentations 1:20-22).

161. Jeremiah for consideration (Lamentations 2:20-22).

162. Jeremiah for judgment (Lamentations 3:55-66).

163. Jeremiah for the oppressed people of Judah (Lamentations 5).

Jeremiah could be called the praying prophet as well as the weeping prophet. He has 15 recorded prayers.

Three Prayers in Ezekiel

164. Ezekiel protesting what God wanted him to do (Ezekiel 4:14).

165. Ezekiel for the remnant (Ezekiel 9:8).

166. Ezekiel for the remnant (Ezekiel 11:13).

Two Prayers in Daniel

167. Daniel for forgiveness of sins and fulfillment of prophecy (Daniel 9:1-19).

168. Daniel for revelation (Daniel 12:8).

References to prayer (Daniel 2:17-18; 6:10).

Two Prayers in Amos

169. Amos for forgiveness (Amos 7:2).

170. Amos for help (Amos 7:5).

Three Prayers in Jonah

171. Sailors for mercy (Jonah 1:14).

172. Jonah for deliverance from hell (Jonah 2:1-9).

173. Jonah for death (Jonah 4:2-3).

Three Prayers in Habakkuk

174. Habakkuk for God to act (Habakkuk 1:1-5).

175. Habakkuk for judgment (Habakkuk 1:12-17).

176. Habakkuk for revival (Habakkuk 3:2-19).

Seventeen Prayers in Matthew

177. Jesus, the Lord's Prayer (Matthew 6:9-13).

178. Leper for healing (Matthew 8:2). Answered (Matthew 8:3).

179. Centurion for healing of his servant (Matthew 8:6-9). Answered (Matthew 8:13).

180. Disciples for help from drowning (Matthew 8:25). Answered (Matthew 8:26).

181. Demons for temporary liberty (Matthew 8:29-31). Answered (Matthew 8:32).

182. A ruler for healing (Matthew 9:18). Answered (Matthew 9:25).

183. A woman for healing (Matthew 9:21). Answered (Matthew 9:22).

184. Two blind men for healing (Matthew 9:27). Answered (Matthew 9:29-30).

185. Jesus giving thanks to God (Matthew 11:25).

186. Peter to walk on water (Matthew 14:28). Answered (Matthew 14:29).

187. Peter for help from drowning (Matthew 14:30). Answered (Matthew 14:31).

188. A woman for healing of her daughter (Matthew 15:22-27). Answered (Matthew 15:28).

189. A man for healing of his son (Matthew 17:15-16). Answered (Matthew 17:18).

190. A mother for exaltation of her 2 sons, James and John (Matthew 20:21). Unanswered because of wrong motive and not in harmony with God's plan (Matthew 20:23).

191. Two blind men for healing (Matthew 20:30-33). Answered (Matthew 20:34).

192. Jesus to be saved from death in the garden before He could die on the cross (62 words; Matthew 26:39-44). Answered (Hebrews 5:7).

193. Jesus on the cross (9 words; Matthew 27:46).

References to prayer (Matthew 6:5-13; 7:7-11; Matthew 14:23; 18:19-20; 21:22; 23:14).

Two Prayers in Mark

194. A demon for temporary freedom (Mark 1:23-24).

195. Jesus in healing a deaf mute (Mark 7:34). Answered (Mark 7:35).

References to prayer (Mark 1:35; 6:41, 46; 9:23; 11:22-24).

Seven Prayers in Luke

196. Simeon in blessing Jesus (Luke 2:29-32).

197. Rich man in hell (Luke 16:24-31).

198. Ten lepers for healing (Luke 17:13). Answered (Luke 17:14, 19).

199. A Pharisee in boasting of his righteousness (Luke 18:11-12). Unjustified (Luke 18:14).

200. A publican for mercy (Luke 18:13). Answered, justified (Luke 18:14).

201. Jesus on the cross (Luke 23:34).

202. Jesus on the cross (Luke 23:46).

References to prayer (Luke 3:21-22; 5:16; 6:12; 9:28-29; 11:1-13; 18:1-18; 22:31-32).

Five Prayers in John

203. Nobleman for healing of child (John 4:49). Answered (John 4:50).

204. People for living bread (John 6:34).

205. Jesus for resurrection of Lazarus (John 11:41-43). Answered (John 11:44).

206. Jesus for glorification (John 12:27-28). Answered (John 12:28).

207. Jesus for disciples (John 17).

References to prayer (John 7:37-39; 14:12-15; 15:7, 16; 16:23-26).

Six Prayers in Acts

208. Disciples for successor to Judas (Acts 1:24-25). Answered (Acts 1:26).

209. Peter for healing of lame man (Acts 3:6). Answered (Acts 3:7-8).

210. Disciples for boldness and power (Acts 4:24-30). Answered (Acts 4:31-33).

211. Stephen for enemies (Acts 7:59-60).

212. Paul for instruction (Acts 9:5-6). Answered (Acts 9:5-6).

213. Peter for resurrection of Tabitha (Acts 9:40). Answered (Acts 9:40-41).

References to prayer (Acts 1:14; 3:1; 6:4; 8:22,24,34; 10:9,31; 12:5; 16:13-16).

One Prayer in 3 John

214. That we the readers would prosper and be in good health as our souls prosper (3 John: 2)

Eight Prayers in Revelation

215. Elders in worship (Revelation 4:11).

216. Angels in worship (Revelation 5:12).

217. All creatures in worship (Revelation 5:13).

218. Martyrs for vengeance (Revelation 6:10).

219. Great multitude in worship (Revelation 7:10).

220. Angels in worship (Revelation 7:12).

221. Glorified saints in worship (Revelation 19:1-6).

222. John for the coming of Jesus Christ a second time, (Revelation 22:20).

Besides the actual worded prayers in these 31 books of the Bible, there are many passages containing no prayers, which give much instruction on the subject of prayer.

It is thought by some that there are a number of prayers in the epistles, but in reality, these books contain only statements to Christians regarding the apostles praying for them that God would bless them, or they give instructions for Christians to pray and tell them what to pray for.

These are not actual prayers addressed to God, however (Romans 1:8-10; 16:20; Ephesians 1:15-20; 3:13-21; Philippians 1:2-7; Colossians 1:3-14; 1 Thessalonians 1:2-3; 3:9-13; 1 Tim 1:3-7; 2 Tim 4:14-18; James 5:13-18).

Thirty-five Books Where a Direct Prayer Is Not Mentioned.

1. Leviticus

2. Ruth

3. Esther

4. Proverbs

5. Ecclesiastes

6. Song of Solomon

7. Hosea

8. Joel

9. Obadiah

10. Micah

11. Nahum

12. Zephaniah

13. Haggai

14. Zechariah

15. Malachi

16. Romans

17. 1 Corinthians

18. 2 Corinthians

19. Galatians

20. Ephesians

21. Philippians

22. Colossians

23. 1 Thessalonians

24. 2 Thessalonians

25. 1 Timothy

26. 2 Timothy

27. Titus

28. Philemon

29. Hebrews

30. James

31. 1 Peter

32. 2 Peter

33. 1 John

34. 2 John

35. Jude[89]

---

[89] https://www.hopefaithprayer.com/prayernew/222-prayers-of-the-bible/

APPENDIX II

Some Christian Quotes on Prayer

I WILL CONCLUDE THIS BOOK WITH QUOTES ON PRAYER FROM SOME PROMINENT MEN AND WOMEN OF GOD.

Be blessed.[90]

"Prayer is a shield to the soul, a sacrifice to God, and a scourge for Satan."- **John Bunyan**

"The fewer the words the better prayer."- **Martin Luther**

---

[90] See, http://www.whatchristianswanttoknow.com/50-christian-prayer-quotes-and-sayings/

"Prayer is an effort of will." - **Oswald Chambers**

"Our prayer and God's mercy are like two buckets in a well; while one ascends, the other descends." - **Arthur Hopkins**

"If sinners be damned, at least let them leap to Hell over our bodies. If they will perish, let them perish with our arms about their knees. Let no one go there unwarned and unprayed for."
- **Charles H. Spurgeon**

"It is because of the hasty and superficial conversation with God that the sense of sin is so weak and that no motives have power to help you to hate and flee from sin as you should." - **A.W. Tozer**

"Prayer is not monologue, but dialogue. God's voice in response to mine is its most essential part." - **Andrew Murray**

"Don't pray when you feel like it. Have an appointment with the Lord and keep it. A man is powerful on his knees. "
- **Corrie Ten Boom**

"Prayer is the acid test of devotion." - **Samuel Chadwick**

"Prayer – secret, fervent, believing prayer – lies at the root of all personal godliness"- **Williams Carey**

"The prayer offered to God in the morning during your quiet time is the key that unlocks the door of the day. Any athlete knows that it is the start that ensures a good finish."- **Adrian Rogers**

"Oh! Yes, (the prayer meeting) is the place to meet with the Holy Ghost, and this is the way to get His mighty power. If we would have Him, we must meet in greater Numbers; we must pray with greater fervency, we must watch with greater earnestness, and believe with firmer steadfastness. The prayer meeting…is the appointed place for the reception of power."- **Charles H. Spurgeon**

"There has never been a spiritual awakening in any country or locality that did not begin in united prayer." - **A.T. Pierson**

"Gentlemen, I have lived a long time and am convinced that God governs in the affairs of men. If a sparrow cannot fall to the ground without His notice, is it probable that an empire can rise without His aid? I move that prayer imploring the assistance of Heaven be held every morning before we proceed to business."- **Benjamin Franklin**

"Shall I give you yet another reason why you should pray? I have preached my very heart out. I could not say any more than I have said. Will not your prayers accomplish that which my preaching fails to do? Is it not likely that the Church has been putting forth its preaching hand but not its praying hand? Oh dear friends! Let us agonize in prayer."- **Charles H. Spurgeon**

"Man who prays much in private will make short prayers in public."
- **D.L. Moody**

"When we become too glib in prayer we are most surely talking to ourselves."- **A.W. Tozer**

"There is neither encouragement nor room in Bible religion for feeble desires, listless efforts, lazy attitudes; all must be strenuous, urgent, ardent desires, impassioned, unwearied insistence delight heaven. God would have His children incorrigibly in earnest and persistently bold in their efforts. Heaven is too busy to listen to half-hearted prayers or to respond to pop-calls. Our whole being must be in our praying."
- **E.M. Bounds**

God loves importunate prayer so much that He will not give us much blessings without it." - **Adoniram Judson**

"If you find your life of prayer to be always so short, and so easy, and so spiritual, as to be without cost and strain and sweat to you, you may depend upon it, you have not yet begun to pray."
- **Alexander Whyte**

"I know of no better thermometer to your spiritual temperature than this, the measure of the intensity of your prayer."
-**Charles H. Spurgeon**

"We can do nothing without prayer. All things can be done by importunate prayer. It surmounts or removes all obstacles, overcomes every resisting force and gains its ends in the face of invincible hindrances."- **E.M. Bounds**

"Prayer is the link that connects us with God."- **A.B. Simpson**

"O, let the place of secret prayer become to me the most beloved spot on earth."- **Andrew Murray**

"Know your HOLY GOD intimately. (When you have seen His glory, His holiness and His love – by drawing close to Him in prayer – then you can usually see through any counterfeits because you know the "real thing" so well)."- **Andrew Strom**

"How different the world would look, how different the state of our nation would be, if there were more sanctified priestly souls! These are souls who have the power to bless, for they intercede with sanctified hearts. They never begin their daily time of intercessory prayer without having first brought to the cross all that is unholy in their lives, so that their old self can be crucified there with Jesus, the sacrificial Lamb."
- **Basilea Schlink**

"A prayerless church member is a hindrance. He is in the body like a rotting bone or a decayed tooth. Before long, since he does not contribute to the benefit of his brethren, he will become a danger and a sorrow to them. Neglect of private prayer is the locust which devours the strength of the church."- **Charles H. Spurgeon**

"The entire day receives order and discipline when it acquires unity. This unity must be sought and found in Morning Prayer. The morning prayer determines the day."- **Dietrich Bonhoeffer**

"No prayer!—No faith!—No Christ in the heart. Little prayer!—Little faith!—Little Christ in the heart. Increasing prayer!—Increasing faith!—Increasing Christ in the heart! Much prayer!—Much faith!—Much Christ in the heart! Praying always!—Faith always!—Christ always!"
-**Alexander Whyte**

"The Prince of the power of the air seems to bend all the force of his attack against the spirit of prayer." - **Andrew Bonar**

"Do not strive in your own strength; cast yourself at the feet of the Lord Jesus, and wait upon Him in the sure confidence that He is with you, and works in you. Strive in prayer; let faith fill your heart-so will you be strong in the Lord, and in the power of His might."
- **Andrew Murray**

"When human reason has exhausted every possibility, the children can go to their Father and receive all they need. ... For only when you have become utterly dependent upon prayer and faith, only when all human possibilities have been exhausted, can you begin to reckon that God will intervene and work His miracles."- **Basilea Schlink**

"The Lord intends us to be powerful people-mighty in optimism and hopeful of spirit, powerful in evangelistic zeal, potent in influence, sturdy in moral fiber and purity. We can be powerhouses in prayer and preaching." - **David Jeremiah**

"If you are strangers to prayer you are strangers to power.
- **Billy Sunday**

"If you want that splendid power in prayer, you must remain in loving, living, lasting, conscious, practical, abiding union with the Lord Jesus Christ." - **Charles H. Spurgeon**

"The prayers of God's saints strengthen the unborn generation against the desolating waves of sin and evil."- **E.M. Mounds**

"A true prayer is an inventory of needs, a catalog of necessities, an exposure of secret wounds, and a revelation of hidden poverty."
- **Charles H. Spurgeon**

"Prayer does not mean that I am to bring God down to my thoughts and my purposes, and bend his government according to my foolish, silly, and sometimes sinful notions. Prayer means that I am to be raised up into feeling, into union and design with him; that I am to enter into his counsel and carry out his purpose fully." -**D.L. Moody**

"Prayer is simply a two-way conversation between you and God."
- **Billy Graham**

IMAGINATIVE PRAYER TEMPLATES

"Prayer is the way you defeat the devil, reach the lost, restore a backslider, strengthen the saints, send missionaries out, cure the sick, accomplish the impossible, and know the will of God."

- **David Jeremiah**

Prayer does not mean simply to pour out one's heart. It means rather to find the way to God and to speak with him, whether the heart is full or empty."- **Dietrich Bonhoeffer**

"Prayer is the easiest and hardest of all things; the simplest and the sublimest; the weakest and the most powerful; its results lie outside the range of human possibilities-they are limited only by the omnipotence of God."- **E.M. Bounds**

"When praying for the Lord's will about something questionable, don't give up if you don't receive clear leading after one prayer; just keep on praying until God makes it clear."- **Curtis Hutson**

"Just as in prayer it is not we who momentarily catch His attention, but He ours, so when we fail to hear His voice, it is not because He is not speaking so much as that we are not listening. We must recognize that all things are in God and that God is in all things, and we must learn to be very attentive, in order to hear God speaking in His ordinary tone without any special accent."- **Charles H. Brent**

Our prayers run along one road and God's answers by another, and by and by they meet."- **Adoniram Judson**

"So don't give up! Don't stop believing! Stay full of hope and expectation. God's power is limitless, and He'll breakthrough for you."- **Joyce Meyer**

"Beware in your prayers, above everything else, of limiting God, not only by unbelief, but by fancying that you know what He can do." - **Andrew Murray**

"I firmly believe a great many prayers are not answered because we are not willing to forgive someone."- **D.L. Moody**

"It matters little what form of prayer we adopt or how many words we use. What matters is the faith which lays hold on God, knowing that He knows our needs before we even ask Him. That is what gives Christian prayer its boundless confidence and its joyous certainty."- **Dietrich Bonhoeffer**

"Prayer does not influence God. Prayer surely does influence God. It does not influence His purpose. It does influence His action." - **S.D. Gordon**[91]

---

[91] See, http://www.whatchristianswanttoknow.com/50-christian-prayer-quotes-and-sayings/

IN CLOSING

If you have been blessed by this book, your comments are welcomed

Please purchase additional copies and give out as gifts. Copies can be purchased from Amazon.com. We want to reach as many people as possible.

You may wish to send a tax deductible donation to aid the work of God. Please e-mail us at CalvaryGatheringMinistry@gmail.com. We will respond to your email with our mailing address to receive your tax deductible gifts.

Blessings.
Rev. Ademola O. Sodeinde

IMAGINATIVE PRAYER TEMPLATES

NOTES

www.ingramcontent.com/pod-product-compliance
Lightning Source LLC
LaVergne TN
LVHW051505070426
835507LV00022B/2935